Weird Birds

CHRIS EARLEY

FIREFLY BOOKS

A Firefly Book

Published by Firefly Books Ltd. 2014
Copyright © 2014 Firefly Books Ltd.
Text copyright © 2014 Chris Earley

First printing

Publisher Cataloging-in-Publication Data (U.S.)
Earley, Chris.
Weird birds / Chris Earley.
[64] p. : col. photos. ; cm.
Includes index.
Summary: Explores the weird and wonderful world of birds through images and descriptions of their behavior and features.
ISBN-13: 978-1-77085-441-3
ISBN-13: 978-1-77085-296-9 (pbk.)
1. Birds – Juvenile literature. 2. Birds – Behavior – Juvenile literature. I. Title.
598 dc23 QL676.2E365 2014

Library and Archives Canada Cataloguing in Publication
Earley, Chris G., 1968-, author
Weird birds / Chris Earley.
Includes index.
ISBN 978-1-77085-441-3 (bound).--ISBN 978-1-77085-296-9 (pbk.)
1. Birds--Juvenile literature. 2. Birds--Behavior--Juvenile literature. I. Title.
QL676.2.E287 2014   j598   C2014-901158-X

Published in the United States by
Firefly Books (U.S.) Inc.
P.O. Box 1338, Ellicott Station
Buffalo, New York 14205

Published in Canada by
Firefly Books Ltd.
50 Staples Avenue, Unit 1
Richmond Hill, Ontario L4B 0A7

IMAGE CREDITS:

Front cover © Rudy Umans / Shutterstock; page 4 © visceralimage / Shutterstock; page 5 © Glenn Bartley / Visuals Unlimited, Inc.; page 6 © Robin Chittenden / naturepl.com; page 7 © Tom Vezo / naturepl.com; page 8 © Buckskinman / Dreamstime.com; page 9 © Rod Williams / naturepl.com; page 10 © Kenneth W. Fink / ardea.com; page 11 © Nick Gordon / naturepl.com; page 12 © Zepherwind / Dreamstime.com; page 13 © Markus Varesvuo; page 14 © phugunfire / Shutterstock; page 15 © Ole Jorgen Liodden / naturepl.com; page 16 © Markus Varesvuo / naturepl.com; page 17 © Arnoud Quanjer / Shutterstock; page 18 © Thomas Marent / Minden Pictures; page 19 © Tim Laman / naturepl.com; page 20 © Roger Powell / naturepl.com ; page 21 © Nagel Photography / Shutterstock; page 22 © Nataliya Hora / Shutterstock; page 23 © FloridaStock / Shutterstock; page 24 © Stubblefield Photography / Shutterstock; page 25 © Gerrit Vyn / naturepl.com; page 26 © Eric Isselee / Shutterstock; page 27 © Christian Musat / Shutterstock; page 28 © Narisa Koryanyong / Shutterstock; page 29 © pandapaw / Shutterstock ; page 30 © gopause / Shutterstock; page 31 © Eric Isselee / Shutterstock; page 32 © Eric Isselee / Shutterstock; page 33 © Eric Isselee / Shutterstock; page 34 © Eric Isselee / Shutterstock; page 35 © Hermann Brehm / naturepl.com; page 36 © Anan Kaewkhammul / Shutterstock; page 37 © Christian Musat / Shutterstock; page 38 © Leksele / Shutterstock; page 39 © Eric Isselee / Shutterstock; page 40 © Mark Bowler / naturepl.com; page 41 © tristan tan / Shutterstock; page 42 © anekoho / Shutterstock; page 43 © Patrick Rolands / Shutterstock; page 44 © hagit berkovich / Shutterstock; page 45 © Eric Isselee / Shutterstock; page 46 © Eric Isselee / Shutterstock; page 47 © Rudy Umans / Shutterstock; page 48 © Stefan Petru Andronache / Shutterstock; page 49 © Eric Isselee / Shutterstock; page 50 © Super Prin / Shutterstock; page 51 © Eric Isselee / Shutterstock; page 52 © Eric Isselee / Shutterstock; page 53 © Andrew Burgess / Shutterstock; page 54–55 © Rosalie Kreulen / Shutterstock; page 56 © Eric Isselee / Shutterstock; page 57 © Oleksiy Mark / Shutterstock; page 58 © Michal Ninger / Shutterstock; page 59 © Christian Vinces / Shutterstock; page 60 © Staffan Widstrand / naturepl.com; page 61 © Dr. Axel Gebauer / naturepl.com; page 62 © veleknez / Shutterstock; page 63 © Tony Heald / naturepl.com; Back cover, right © phugunfire / Shutterstock; Back cover, left © Arnoud Quanjer / Shutterstock.

The publisher gratefully acknowledges the financial support for our publishing program by the Government of Canada through the Canada Book Fund as administered by the Department of Canadian Heritage.

Cover and interior design by Jacqueline Hope Raynor

Printed in China

INTRODUCTION

When most people first think of birds, they think of pigeons or sparrows or maybe the pretty cardinal at their backyard bird feeder. But when you start to tally the many different kinds of birds you know, you realize how diverse and amazing these vertebrates are. From massive flightless ostriches to tiny whirring hummingbirds, birds come in all sorts of shapes and sizes. And the size range is impressive: it would take 67,650 bee hummingbirds, often regarded as the world's smallest bird, to reach the weight of the world's heaviest bird, the ostrich.

Birds are the only modern creatures to possess feathers. Feathers grow from follicles in the skin (like mammalian hairs do) and they are made up of keratin, which is also found in claws and scales. It is likely that feathers evolved from reptilian scales. Feathers are what allow birds to fly, along with other adaptations such as being light (hollow bones, no teeth, smaller or loss of organs) and powerful (strong breast muscles). Feathers also help birds stay warm and waterproof. But their function in visual communication is something that really makes birdlife so spectacular.

Feathers come in an incredible variety of colors and shapes for the purpose of attracting a mate, but this attracts our attention as well. The massive tail of a peacock, the rainbow colors of a parrot or the fine plumes of an egret have been impressing people for thousands of years.

But it is not just feathers that make birds strange to us. The different shapes of birds make them an especially diverse group of animals. Pondering beaks alone, there are the dagger-like beaks of herons, the curved beaks of ibises and the hooked beaks of owls and hawks. Other beaks are shaped as chisels, spoons, probes, tweezers, sieves and pouches. Legs and feet are almost as variable. Long legs of storks, webbed feet of ducks, skinny toes of jacanas and weapon-like claws of raptors help birds find and secure food. The plethora of beaks and leg shapes are just a few of the adaptations that help birds survive in habitats all over the planet.

With over 10,000 species, birds are sure to impress anyone who stops to take a closer look.

BLACK SKIMMER

Rynchops niger

The skimmer may have the strangest beak in the world. The bird flies very low, just above a pond or river, and pushes its abnormally long lower beak (called a mandible) through the surface of the water. When it hits a fish or other prey, it clamps the upper mandible down and has its meal. All weird beaks have a distinct and usually fascinating purpose.

BOOTED RACKET-TAIL

Ocreatus underwoodii
The tail of the male Booted Racket-tail allows this tiny bird to make its speedy flight incredibly fascinating. As the bird flies from flower to flower, the large circles at the end of its two long tail feathers follow along on beautiful display. This hummingbird is found in the Andes of South America.

BROWN-WINGED KINGFISHER

Pelargopsis amauroptera

There are over 90 species of kingfishers and most of them have really big beaks for the size of their bodies. Many species catch fish with these spear-like beaks and some are able to dive from the air to over 6 feet beneath the water's surface to find food. But some kingfisher species do a lot of hunting away from water where they catch insects, frogs, toads, lizards and even small mammals.

BLUE-FOOTED BOOBY

Sula nebouxii

Blue-footed Boobies have a complex courtship display that focuses on showing off their brilliantly blue feet. During the courtship, they lift their feet in an exaggerated walk and flaunt them for all the females to see.

LUZON BLEEDING-HEART PIGEON

Gallicolumba luzonica

Sometimes the coloring of a bird makes it look different. This well-named pigeon appears to have been shot in the chest! The male Luzon Bleeding-heart puffs out his breast at a female to display his "heart" during courtship. There are four closely-related species of bleeding-heart pigeon that also display red (or sometimes orange) patches on their breasts.

BROWN EARED-PHEASANT

Crossoptilon mantchuricum
Many male pheasants are spectacular-looking birds while the females are duller and plain. But with all three species of eared-pheasants, both the males and females look the same and that means they both have the characteristic big white moustaches. This species is found in northern China.

CAPUCHINBIRD

Perissocephalus tricolor
This rainforest bird not only looks weird, it sounds weird. The male makes a loud sound that is somewhat similar to a cow mooing, giving these birds their other common name: Calfbird. The males group together and compete for attention from the females with their calls. So, if you hear what sounds like a herd of cows up in a tree on your next rainforest walk, you may have come across some Capuchinbirds.

BULWER'S PHEASANT

Lophura bulweri
The impressive tail display of a male Bulwer's Pheasant is enhanced
with its wacky royal blue wattles and horns. These blue adornments
are usually small and inconspicuous, but during the mating display
the male extends the wattles and horns to impress his potential mate.

SOUTHERN SCREAMER

Chauna torquata

Though it looks more like an overgrown chicken, the Southern Screamer of South America is actually more closely related to geese and ducks. It has partially webbed feet and can swim rather well. It gets its name from the loud, far-carrying scream that it makes.

RED CROSSBILL

Loxia curvirostra
The awesome beak of the Red Crossbill
is used to open pine cones to get at the
seeds inside. Some of these birds are
righties and some are lefties depending on
how their beak is crossed. Birds with their
lower mandible curved to the left, usually
hold the pine cone with their right foot and
vice versa. This likely makes their foraging as
efficient as possible.

SOUTHERN CASSOWARY

Casuarius casuarius
This large flightless rainforest bird is the second
heaviest bird in the world after the ostrich. And the
female cassowary is larger and more colorful than
her mate: she can weigh up to 130 pounds. Not only
that, after she lays her eggs she leaves the male to
incubate them and raise the young on his own.

FRIGATEBIRD

Fregata sp.

Male frigatebirds can inflate their throat sacs into huge red balloons that really impress the female frigatebirds. The male inflates his sac and moves it back and forth at females that fly by. They also do a special call during this display that sounds a bit like a science fiction ray gun!

KING EIDER

Somateria spectabilis
Related to the Common Eider, which is famous for providing us with soft down used in pillows and quilts, the male King Eider distinguishes himself with his bulbous and colorful head. Only a handful of the world's bird species breed as far north as this Arctic duck, which can nest on the northern coast of Ellesmere Island.

SOUTHERN GROUND HORNBILL

Bucorvus leadbeateri
Note the contrast between the
Southern Ground Hornbill's grotesque
facial skin and its elegant long
eyelashes. This turkey-sized hornbill
hunts by walking through the African
savannah and grabbing insects,
snakes, lizards and small mammals
with its large beak.

17

RESPLENDENT QUETZAL

Pharomachrus mocinno
The intense beauty of this bird has
been noticed by many cultures in
many eras. It was revered as sacred
by the Aztecs and Maya, who used
its beautiful, long tail feathers
(taken from live-caught birds that
were then released) in ceremonial
headdresses. It is Guatemala's
national bird and also the name of
Guatemala's currency.

RED BIRD-OF-PARADISE

Paradisaea rubra
The Birds-of-Paradise are a family of
birds that include some of the world's
most beautiful and bizarre creatures.
Incredibly ornate feathers on the males
of different species are used during
elaborate courtship displays. The Red
Bird-of-Paradise uses his long feathers to
frame his upside down display.

19

RUFF

Philomachus pugnax
The most flamboyant of the sandpipers, the breeding male Ruff lives up to his name with a profusion of elongated neck and head feathers. These feathers can be white, black or rufous brown. The males group together and show off their magnificent feathers to females that come to choose a mate.

INCA TERN

Larosterna inca
Both male and female Inca Terns have curly face feathers. This seabird is found on the west coast of South America where it breeds on islands and rocky cliff faces. Those that nest on islands are threatened by rats and cats introduced to the islands by humans.

SHOEBILL

Balaeniceps rex
Named for the shape of its beak,
this heron-like bird appears to be
carrying a wooden Dutch shoe on its
face. The Shoebill uses this massive
beak to catch a wide variety of prey
including fish, amphibians, snakes,
young ducks, small mammals and
even baby crocodiles.

ROSEATE SPOONBILL

Platalea ajaja

There are six species of spoonbill in the world, but the Roseate Spoonbill is the only one that is bright pink. All of them have beaks shaped like a spoon that they use to catch prey. The swollen end of the beak is opened slightly and moved back and forth in the water until it touches a fish or other prey. Then the beak snaps shut and the spoonbill swallows its catch.

ANHINGA

Anhinga anhinga
This bird is also called the snakebird
because of its long neck. This neck allows
the Anhinga to submerge itself in the
water with only its head showing. It
then slowly paddles forward and goes
underwater completely to hunt for fish
that it spears with its sharp beak.

GREATER SAGE-GROUSE

Centrocercus urophasianus

This male grouse seems to be showing off his ample bosom, but really he has inflated two sacs on his throat just like the frigatebird does. Like the Ruff, the grouse uses these sacs to compete with other males to win the attention of a female. He uses them to make a strange echoing sound that carries across his prairie home to any females in the area.

SCARLET IBIS

Eudocimus ruber

The Scarlet Ibis is one of 26 different ibis species and all of them have a droopy beak. They eat a wide variety of prey including insects, crabs, shrimp and fish. Scarlet Ibis have been known to follow feeding ducks and grazing cows to eat the insects that these animals scare out of hiding.

SACRED IBIS

Threskiornis aethiopicus
Another member of the ibis family, the
Sacred Ibis is found in much of Africa
south of the Sahara Desert. This species
eats even more different food items
than most ibises and can even be found
foraging for scraps at garbage dumps.

BLUE-TAILED BEE-EATER

Merops philippinus
Bee-eaters live up to their name by eating
many flying insects including stinging ones
such as wasps and bees. Before they
swallow a wasp or bee, they rub it
on a branch to get rid of the
stinger and squeeze out
the insect's venom.

AMERICAN FLAMINGO

Phoenicopterus ruber
Flamingoes are one of the most recognizable
of birds. They often have pink plumage and
they have been immortalized as a plastic
lawn ornament. Real flamingoes feed by
dipping their bent beaks upside down in the
water and filtering out the tiny organisms
that serve as food and that also give them
their pink coloration. Though they look
more like a heron or a stork, flamingoes may
actually be more closely related to grebes.

ASIAN PARADISE-FLYCATCHER

Terpsiphone paradisi

A male Asian Paradise-Flycatcher has an incredibly long tail. When the male is young, its tail is short like that of a female, but when it becomes an adult, its tail grows so much that it more than doubles the bird's total length. This species can be found in many color variations and some individuals are almost all white with black heads.

ATLANTIC PUFFIN

Fratercula arctica

The clown of the seabird world, the Atlantic
Puffin's very colorful beak has tiny spines
along the inside part of the upper mandible.
These spines, as well as those found on
the bird's tongue, allow the puffin to
carry up to 50 small fish back from
the sea to the burrow containing
the puffin's young.

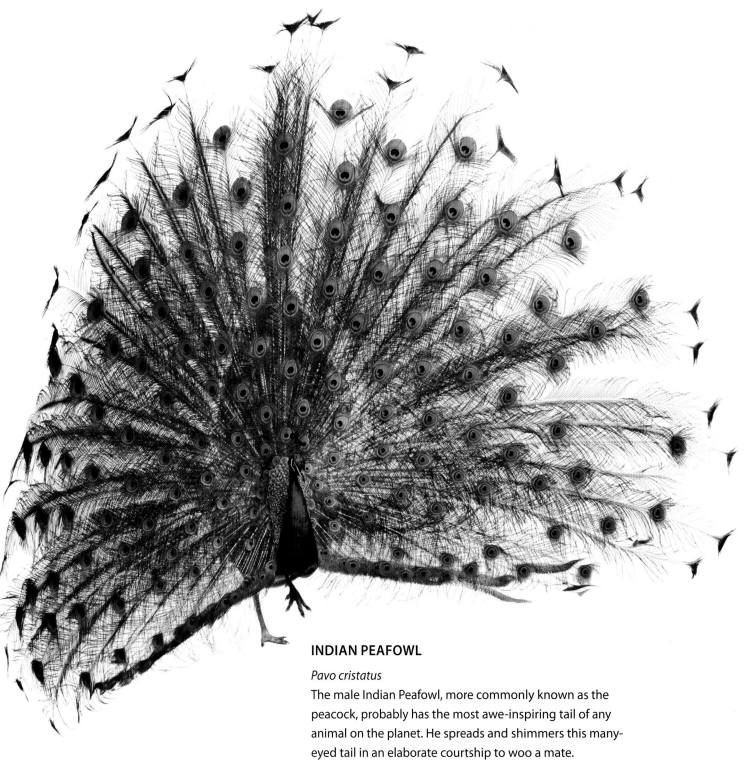

INDIAN PEAFOWL

Pavo cristatus

The male Indian Peafowl, more commonly known as the peacock, probably has the most awe-inspiring tail of any animal on the planet. He spreads and shimmers this many-eyed tail in an elaborate courtship to woo a mate.

MACAWS

There are 16 species of large, long-tailed parrots called macaws. These colorful birds, often used as symbols of the rainforest, are sometimes seen in large, noisy flocks. Unfortunately, the macaw's impressive size and colors has made it a target for poaching for the pet trade.

NORTH ISLAND BROWN KIWI

Apteryx mantelli
Like the ostrich, this is another flightless bird. But, while the
ostrich lays the smallest egg in relation to body size of any bird
(about 2%), the female kiwi lays an egg that weighs an incredible
one quarter (25%) of her total body weight!

CHESTNUT-EARED ARACARI

Pteroglossus castanotis
Aracaris are small toucans that live in Central and South America. Their main diet is fruit and they often regurgitate the seeds. One study found that 96% of these seeds were viable, showing that aracaris are probably important seed dispersers in the rain forest.

OSTRICH

Struthio camelus

This is the largest bird in the world. It can weigh over 400 pounds and stand over 6.5 feet tall. The ostrich does lay the largest egg in the world (about the same as 24 chicken eggs), but it is the smallest bird egg in relation to the bird's body size.

GREATER RHEA

Rhea americana
While ostriches live in Africa, rheas live
in South America. They are not as big as
ostriches, but at 5 feet tall, they are still large
birds. Up to 12 female rheas lay their eggs in
one nest and a single male incubates them.
There can be up to 60 eggs in a single nest!

KING PENGUIN

Aptenodytes patagonicus
Penguins are one of the most distinctive bird groups in the world. They don't fly, but use their wings to swim underwater instead. They can swim over 20 miles per hour to catch fish, squid and crustaceans. Their speed also gives them a chance of outmaneuvering predators such as Killer Whales, Leopard Seals and sharks.

HUMBOLDT PENGUIN

Spheniscus humboldti

Penguins and other seabirds that live in salt water have to be able get rid of the excess salt that builds up in their systems. These birds have salt glands located above their eyes that extract the excess salt from their bodies and dribbles it as a liquid out of the birds' nostrils.

ROYAL FLYCATCHER

Onychorhynchus coronatus

Most flycatchers are rather dull, but this species has a spectacular crest of colorful feathers. The crest is usually folded up behind the bird's head and its exact function has yet to be discovered. When caught by scientists, the bird unfolds its crest and moves his head from side to side very slowly, suggesting that the crest may be used in some kind of threat display.

HELMETED GUINEAFOWL

Numida meleagris

The bald heads, upright casques and wrinkly wattles of the Helmeted Guineafowl make these chicken-like birds very eye-catching. But these adornments are not just for beauty. All of the bare skin helps the guineafowl regulate its brain temperature in a variety of different African climatic conditions.

HORNBILLS

Bucerotidae

This family of birds is found in Africa and southern Asia. Their massive beaks are characteristic of all members of the family. Some species, like the birds shown here, have beaks that are decorated with large, colorful casques. Like the South American toucans, some hornbill species are probably important seed dispersers of many different fruit-bearing trees. For protection, most female hornbills seal themselves and their eggs into tree cavities with a mixture of mud and feces. A small opening is left in the mud wall so the male can feed the female and young until it is time to break them out.

GOLDEN PHEASANT

Chrysolophus pictus

The male Golden Pheasant of China has a strange display tactic. When he wants to impress a female pheasant, he runs up to her and fans one side of his gold and black neck ruff up in front of her face. He then turns and does the other side. The male repeats this behavior in hopes that the female will accept it as a mate.

EURASIAN EAGLE-OWL

Bubo bubo

Almost everything about an owl is weird, mostly because it is one of the only bird groups in the world that is primarily nocturnal. Owls have adapted to their night-time hunting schedule with huge light-sensitive eyes, incredibly acute hearing and very quiet flight that helps them sneak up on their prey in the dark.

PALM COCKATOO

Probosciger aterrimus
Besides having a very impressive "hairdo", the Palm Cockatoo has a talent that is unique in the bird world. The male is a drummer. He fashions a drumstick out of a branch and then bangs it against a hollow tree trunk so the sound echoes through his territory. This musical solo is used to attract a mate.

BROWN PELICAN

Pelecanus occidentalis

Pelicans use their large, net-like beaks to capture fish and then strain out the water before they swallow their catch. Many species do this as they swim around on the water surface. Brown Pelicans, however, can catch their fish by flying above the water and then doing a spectacular plunge beak-first into an unsuspecting school of fish.

DOMESTIC CHICKENS

Gallus domesticus

Domestication by humans has produced
our most important food bird: the chicken.
By selecting for certain traits, we have taken
the ancestral Red Junglefowl and produced
birds that are heavier and lay more and bigger
eggs. There are hundreds of breeds of chicken
around the world. Some are better for producing
eggs, some for producing meat and some are
fancy breeds that are bred for how ornamental
they look. As you can see by looking at the birds
on these two pages, we have also produced some
very funny-looking chickens!

EURASIAN HOOPOE

Upupa epops

This odd-looking bird has an even odder way of defending itself as a nestling. If it feels threatened, it will spray feces at the potential predator. If that doesn't work, it may hiss, poke the predator with its beak or excrete a stinky substance from its preen gland.

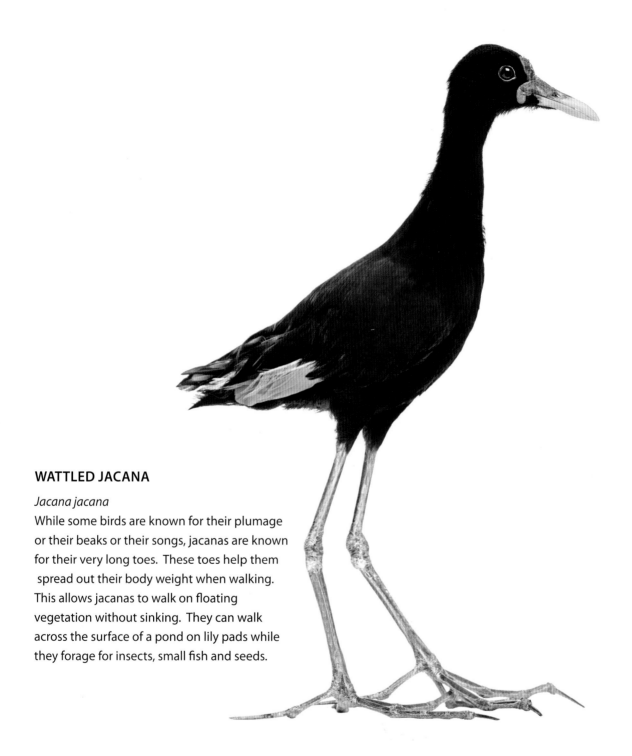

WATTLED JACANA

Jacana jacana
While some birds are known for their plumage or their beaks or their songs, jacanas are known for their very long toes. These toes help them spread out their body weight when walking. This allows jacanas to walk on floating vegetation without sinking. They can walk across the surface of a pond on lily pads while they forage for insects, small fish and seeds.

MARABOU STORK

Leptoptilos crumeniferus
Not only does this bird look like an overgrown, long-billed vulture, it eats like one, too. The Marabou Stork frequently competes with vultures for parts of the carcasses of dead animals. It also eats refuse at garbage dumps, fish and insects.

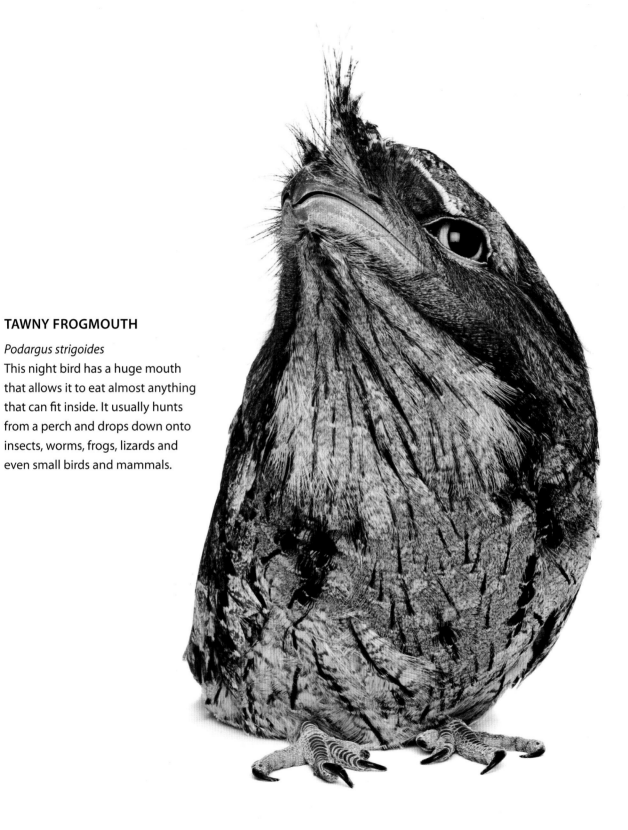

TAWNY FROGMOUTH

Podargus strigoides

This night bird has a huge mouth that allows it to eat almost anything that can fit inside. It usually hunts from a perch and drops down onto insects, worms, frogs, lizards and even small birds and mammals.

SWORD-BILLED HUMMINGBIRD

Ensifera ensifera
The award for longest beak in relation to body size goes
to the Sword-billed Hummingbird. This long beak allows
it to gather nectar from very deep flowers. Unfortunately,
such a long beak makes preening a bit of a problem, so
this hummingbird does a lot of its feather maintenance
with its feet.

SUNBITTERN

Eurypyga helias

The Sunbittern is quite well camouflaged until it feels threatened and does its frontal display by spreading both of its wings and facing the threat. This makes it look much bigger than normal and may scare the intruder away with the large, colorful eye-like pattern on its wings.

TOCO TOUCAN

Ramphastos toco
This toucan has the largest beak of any toucan species. While it is an awkward appendage to haul around, the toucan uses it in a variety of ways. The beak can be used to gather fruit, excavate a nest hole in decaying wood, or steal an egg or nestling from the deep pouched nest of a neighboring bird.

SECRETARYBIRD

Sagittarius serpentarius
Probably the strangest-shaped raptor in
the world, the Secretarybird looks more like
a stork than an eagle. But it does still use
its feet to catch its prey. This species walks
along the African savannah looking for
snakes, lizards, insects and small mammals.
When it finds one, it stomps on its prey
with its strong feet and then, in most cases,
swallows it whole.

ANDEAN COCK-OF-THE-ROCK

Rupicola peruvianus
This brilliant creature is the national bird of
Peru. The bright orange male Andean Cocks-of-the-
Rock display in groups. At these courtship arenas,
the males try to be the best at energetic flapping,
bowing and jumping as well as loud calling, all in the
hopes of attracting one of the female onlookers.

WHITE-HEADED VULTURE

Trigonoceps occipitalis
It is thought that most vultures have featherless heads because it is easier to keep them clean. As carrion eaters, they often stick their heads into carcasses while feeding. Whatever the reason, the bald birds do seem a bit sinister-looking.

TEMMINCK'S TRAGOPAN

Tragopan temminckii

The shiny blue and red of this bird's lappet is what the Temminck's Tragopan uses as a badge of masculinity during his courtship display. He extends the lappet down his breast and inflates two blue horns on his head. He then does some quick head-bobbing and wing flaps and finishes off by standing as tall as he can with his wings extended.

WILD TURKEY

Meleagris gallopavo

Turkeys are well-known birds, but have
you ever really stopped to look closely at one? The red and blue facial
skin in conjunction with the multiple wattles, warts and bumps is quite
bizarre. This head in combination with the chest tuft, huge fan-like tail
and rotund body surely make this one of our weirdest birds.

VULTURINE GUINEAFOWL

Acryllium vulturinum

Another species of guineafowl, the Vulturine Guineafowl is found in dry areas of eastern Africa. It gets its name from having a naked head like that of a vulture. This head, with its Friar Tuck haircut, seems much too small for the bird's body and its suit of stripes and spots make this a very comical-looking bird indeed.

INDEX

American Flamingo *Phoenicopterus ruber* 29

Andean Cock-of-the-Rock *Rupicola peruvianus* 59

Anhinga *Anhinga anhinga* 24

Asian Paradise-flycatcher *Terpsiphone paradisi* 30

Atlantic Puffin *Fratercula arctica* 31

Black Skimmer *Rynchops niger* 4

Blue-footed Booby *Sula nebouxii* 7

Blue-tailed Bee-eater *Merops philippinus* 28

Booted Racket-tail *Ocreatus underwoodii* 5

Brown Eared-pheasant *Crossoptilon mantchuricum* 9

Brown Pelican *Pelecanus occidentalis* 47

Brown-winged Kingfisher *Pelargopsis amauroptera* 6

Bulwers Pheasant *Lophura bulweri* 11

calfbird *see* Capuchinbird

Capuchinbird *Perissocephalus tricolor* 10

Chestnut-eared Aracari *Pteroglossus castanotis* 35

Domestic Chickens *Gallus domesticus* 48-49

Eurasian Eagle-Owl *Bubo bubo* 45

Eurasian Hoopoe *Upupa epops* 50

Frigatebird *Fregata* sp. 15

Golden Pheasant *Chrysolophus pictus* 44

Greater Rhea *Rhea americana* 37

Greater Sage-Grouse *Centrocercus urophasianus* 25

Helmeted Guineafowl *Numida meleagris* 41

Hornbills *Bucerotidae* 42-43

Humboldt Penguin *Spheniscus humboldti* 39

Inca Tern *Larosterna inca* 21

Indian Peafowl *Pavo cristatus* 32

King Eider *Somateria spectabilis* 16

King Penguin *Aptenodytes patagonicus* 38

Luzon Bleeding-heart Pigeon *Gallicolumba luzonica* 8

Macaws 33

Marabou Stork *Leptoptilos crumeniferus* 52

North Island Brown Kiwi *Apteryx mantelli* 34

Ostrich *Struthio camelus* 36

Palm Cockatoo *Probosciger aterrimus* 46

peacock *see* Indian Peafowl

Red Bird-of-Paradise *Paradisaea rubra* 19

Red Crossbill *Loxia curvirostra* 13

Resplendent Quetzal *Pharomachrus mocinno* 18

Roseate Spoonbill *Platalea ajaja* 23

Royal Flycatcher *Onychorhynchus coronatus* 40

Ruff *Philomachus pugnax* 20

Sacred Ibis *Threskiornis aethiopicus* 27

Scarlet Ibis *Eudocimus ruber* 26

Secretarybird *Sagittarius serpentarius* 58

Shoebill *Balaeniceps rex* 22

snakebird *see* Anhinga

Southern Cassowary *Casuarius casuarius* 14

Southern Ground Hornbill *Bucorvus leadbeateri* 17

Southern Screamer *Chauna torquata* 12

Sunbittern *Eurypyga helias* 56

Sword-billed Hummingbird *Ensifera ensifera* 54

Tawny Frogmouth *Podargus strigoides* 53

Temminck's Tragopan *Tragopan temminckii* 61

Toco Toucan *Ramphastos toco* 57

Vulturine Guineafowl *Acryllium vulturinum* 63

Wattled Jacana *Jacana jacana* 51

White-headed Vulture *Trigonoceps occipitalis* 60

Wild Turkey *Meleagris gallopavo* 62